Take All
The Time You Need

Take All the Time You Need

a gift of poetry
to help humans heal
through our shared grief

By Sandy Lender

IYF PUBLISHING/DRAGON HOARD PRESS

Copyright 2024 by Sandy Lender

All rights reserved.

No part of this book may be reproduced in any form or by any electronic or mechanical means, including information storage and/or retrieval systems, without written permission from the author, except for the use of brief quotations in a book review.

LARGE PRINT EDITIONS
Paperback ISBN: 9798990908208
Hardcover ISBN: 9798990908215

IYF Publishing/Dragon Hoard Press
Florida
www.SandyLenderInk.com

Dedication

For Petri

and
all the loved ones
we'll see again...

Introduction

Hopefully each person who comes to this book during a time of grief knows that we all require *whatever* we require to get through this deeply personal emotion. Over three decades ago, a co-worker and I were listening to a colleague share a story of her late husband. His passing, although a few years in the past, was fresh in Barb's heart, and she asked us, "Do you know how long it takes to get over grief?"

My twenty-two-year-old brain thought it a strange question.

Luckily, my co-worker responded before I could fumble anything trite, and he said, "It takes as long as it takes."

    Not only his answer, but also Barb's relieved and hopeful demeanor have stayed with me all these years. When recovering from the losses of grandparents, colleagues, mentors, and friends, it has been a blessing to remember, my grief is allowed to take as long as long as I need it to take. I can take as long as I need to work through grief—for it to be part of my existence.

We are humans and we are supposed to experience emotions. Grief is one of them. Thank God we have one another to lean on, to share this overwhelming burden when it's our turn to experience it.

In 2018, I experienced a loss unlike anything I'd felt before. My companion parrot, Petri, whom I'd raised from a fledgling and who'd been at my side for nineteen years—through job losses and gains; through a divorce then a tumultuous, abusive relationship; through two bouts with cancer; through a move across a country; through financial devastation and hard-fought recovery; through laughter and tears; through funny times and sorrows—had an unexpected seizure on Saturday, September 15. I endured that morning alone at the veterinary clinic when his doctor told me I needed to let him go.

  I still grieve.

  But there are better days now than that horrible autumn of 2018 and the first Christmas without him. I am a follower of Christ and I believe the promises of the Bible. I believe Petri is already in his restored state in eternity, and I know I'll recognize his spirit one day on the other side.

I have heard the derisive comments from online trolls. I've shrugged off the insensitive lack of understanding from people who don't know any better. And I want to share with my fellow humans that each one of us who experiences grief experiences a valid, true emotion that will take as much time to move through and absorb into your existence, as you need it to take.

May this poem be a gift to walk you through a difficult time. May it be a reassurance to you that bright days will dawn again. And may you find in these pages a kindred soul who knows a measure of the pain you know, and who reaches out to touch your hand in commiseration and empathy and kindness.

Thank you for sharing together,
Sandy Lender

Take All
The Time You Need

I cannot manage this pain

cannot lift my head
from salty, saturated pillows
and week-old pajamas
that reek of my unwashed body
and emotional heaving

I cannot eat

for grief steals my food
back from me
leaves the dishes dirty
beside the sink
prevents me making up the bed
or taking the unopened mail from
the table to the trash
overflowing beside the back door

and mocks me for each and every
moment I wasted
on such mundane tasks
when you were still by my side

"We're too young for this,"
a friend wept in commiseration
swatting a fly near the heaped can

I fully agree with her

but at what age
    will it be acceptable
        to watch one you love

sigh out his final breath

some ridiculous,
heartless person
(whose name is now lost to me)
told me how insensitive I am

    how *stupid* of me

to mourn the loss of a pet
when there are families
in the world
who have suffered

    real losses

I cut that person from my life
Get thee away from me, Satan.
Pack up your lack of empathy
Take it somewhere else

for I know the fall into the
fathomless pit
when a companion
of nineteen years
Must let go

    Must let go

        Must let go

and I know the fall into the depths
of despair
when a friend should be letting
tears flow

    over a parent

        over a spouse

            over a child

    over a friend

        over a pet

no one is any less heartbreaking
than another
when it's your turn to grieve
when it's a piece of your heart that
Must let go

    Must let go

        Must let go

I have felt the cord pull taut
and rip loose the sinew
from my bones
    until I bled
        inwardly
from a thorned wound wrapping
itself around my organs

      squeezing the breath
        out of me

I have sat in the dark

welcoming the lightning flash

if only so the thunder crash
might offer noise

to drown the sound of my sobbing

my groaning

my moaning in misery

at the burnt taste of absence

this is the human experience
we all inevitably share
to know love and grief
to take whatever length
of days or years the lungs
require to refill with air
and breathe again

You will breathe again.

and this is the human experience
I am honored to speak
against your ear
softly
with whispered words
with assurance
for the mourning
will pass and the storm
will pass and the thunder
will quiet his raging roll
leaving you with calm
with tender thoughts
on a sun-soaked morn

The sun will shine
on you again.

and this is the human experience
we stand ready to face together
offering patience
peace
understanding
when an unexpected scent
of vanilla bean
whiffs an unexpected medicine
memory
too unexpectedly to the surface
and we break down
like heat-thunder crashing
out of nowhere
on a sweltering afternoon

Oh, let me assure you
with patience
with peace
with understanding

Oh, let me assure you...
these breakdowns will come fewer
and farther in between

I can assure you...
smiles will come more often to your mouth once again tasting pomegranate juice and tart apples

let it ride, this grief,
as long as it must

let it mount its journey along hills and valleys up mountainsides and on trickling creeks of never-ending waters

let it take all the time you require of it

until one day, the grief, you will find, you have learned to cradle in your most healthful hold

through the grief, you will find,
you have learned to manage pain
and sense yourself warmed by
sweet memories again

You will smile
at sweet memories again.

Other Poetry by Sandy Lender

Poems of Trials, Triumphs, and Turtles (2020)
(the 2021 IMADJINNS Best Poetry of the Year by a single author)

Poems of Fact, Form, and Fantasy (2022)

Petals of Haiku: an anthology, edited by Gabriela Marie Milton (2024)

About the Author

Sandy Lender is an international best-selling poet and award-winning author of fantasy, literary fiction, poetry, and short story work.
    She's a construction magazine editor by day and author of #GirlPower fantasy novels by night, living in Florida to help with sea turtle conservation and parrot rescue. You can follow her author page on Amazon at Sandy Lender, check her website at SandyLenderInk.com, or subscribe to her free author newsletter at bit.ly/SSReNews.
    With a four-year degree in English and thirty-year career in publishing, Sandy's successes include traditionally and self-published

novels, hundreds of magazine articles, multiple short stories in competitive anthologies, a handful of technical writing awards, a handful of creative writing awards, and the 2023 Michael Knost Wings award.

   Sandy's been writing stories since she was knee-high to a grasshopper when her great-grandmother shared her odd little tales of squeaky ghost-spiders around an apartment complex in Southern Illinois. The stories have developed to include strong young ladies working with dragons to save worlds from terrible fates, but those pesky spiders still show up from time to time.

   There's always something brewing at Sandy Lender Ink headquarters where *some days, you just want the dragon to win.*

Other Works by Sandy Lender

The CHOICES series
Choices Meant for Gods (book 1)
Choices Meant for Kings (book 2)
Choices Meant for All (book 3)

The DRAGONS IN SPACE series
YA sci-fi/fantasy (3 titles)

The FAERIE HOLIDAYS series
Paranormal vampire-satire (3 titles)

Move the Stars
Destination Premeditation
Dream Crystal for Christmas
She's Not Broken (Kelsey Day)
How to Train Your Human:
a Guide for Parrots
100 Things Duran Duran Fans Should Know & Do During This Life

(and more...)

Thank you
for being a reader.

www.ingramcontent.com/pod-product-compliance
Lightning Source LLC
Chambersburg PA
CBHW031508040426
42444CB00007B/1255